Contents

第一章　共和国勋章获得者 …………… 1
第二章　钟家的长子 …………………… 3
第三章　调皮的男孩 …………………… 8
第四章　重大的选择 …………………… 13
第五章　甜蜜的婚姻 …………………… 17
第六章　艰苦的岁月 …………………… 21
第七章　重回医疗领域 ………………… 25
第八章　迎难而上 ……………………… 29
第九章　海外求学 ……………………… 33
第十章　非典袭来 ……………………… 40
第十一章　敢医敢言 …………………… 46

第十二章　不断进步 ······ 53

第十三章　再战新冠 ······ 58

Chapter One　Winner of the Medal of the Republic ······ 65

Chapter Two　The Eldest Son of the Zhong Family ······ 68

Chapter Three　A Naughty Boy ······ 72

Chapter Four　A Crucial Choice ······ 76

Chapter Five　A Sweet Marriage ······ 80

Chapter Six　Hard Years ······ 84

Chapter Seven　Serving as a Doctor Again ······ 87

Chapter Eight　Rising to the Challenge ······ 91

Chapter Nine　Studying Abroad ······ 95

Chapter Ten　Fighting SARS ······ 103

The Pioneers of Contemporary China
中国时代先锋人物

钟南山
Zhong Nanshan

刘小琳　编著
卢　敏　翻译

First Edition　2021

Fourth Printing　2023

ISBN 978-7-5138-2099-8
Copyright 2021 by Sinolingua Co., Ltd
Published by Sinolingua Co., Ltd
24 Baiwanzhuang Street, Beijing 100037, China
Tel: (86) 10-68320585 68997826
Fax: (86) 10-68997826 68326333
http://www.sinolingua.com.cn
E-mail: hyjx@sinolingua.com.cn
Facebook: www.facebook.com/sinolingua
Printed by Beijing Hucais Culture Communication Co., Ltd

Printed in the People's Republic of China

Chapter Eleven　Daring to Give Honest and Accurate Medical Information ·································· 109

Chapter Twelve　Constantly Making Progress ·································· 116

Chapter Thirteen　Fighting the COVID-19 Epidemic ······················ 121

第一章
共和国勋章获得者

2020年9月8日上午，中国抗击新冠肺炎疫情表彰大会在北京人民大会堂隆重举行。大会对中国在抗击新冠肺炎疫情期间表现突出并做出巨大贡献的优秀个人和集体给予表彰奖励。

一位84岁高龄的老人神采奕奕地迈着坚定的步伐上台领奖，他就是共和国勋章[①]获得者——钟南山。

国家主席习近平亲自为钟南山授勋。当钟南山佩戴上金光灿灿的共和国勋章时，全

[①] 共和国勋章是中华人民共和国最高荣誉勋章，授予在中国特色社会主义建设和保卫国家中做出巨大贡献、建立卓越功勋的杰出人士。

场响起经久不息的掌声。

钟南山到底是什么人？他为何能获此殊荣？

钟南山是中国工程院院士、广州医科大学附属第一医院国家呼吸系统疾病临床医学研究中心主任。新冠肺炎疫情发生后，钟南山敢医敢言，提出存在"人传人"现象，强调严格防控，领导撰写新冠肺炎诊疗方案，在疫情防控、重症救治、科研攻关等方面做出了杰出贡献。

他在获奖发言时说："'健康所系，性命相托'，就是我们医者的初心；保障人民群众的身体健康和生命安全，就是我们医者的使命。"

在2003年的非典型肺炎疫情和这次新冠肺炎疫情两次危机关头，钟南山都用自己的实际行动履行了医者的初心和使命，赢得了全中国人民的爱戴和敬仰。

第二章
钟家的长子

1936年10月20日,钟南山出生在南京中央医院。因为中央医院坐落于南京钟山的南面,父亲钟世藩就给孩子取了"南山"这个的名字。

钟南山的父亲钟世藩出生于1901年,因父母早亡,他从小由叔叔带大。钟世藩一边给人打工一边努力学习,最终以优异的成绩考入了北京协和医学院。毕业后,他又去美国纽约州立大学留学,在1930年拿到了医学博士学位。钟世藩历任南京和贵阳中央医院儿科主任、湘雅医学院儿科教授、广州中央医院院长兼儿科主任、岭南大学医学院

儿科教授兼主任、广州中山医学院儿科教授兼主任。

钟南山的母亲廖月琴也是一位优秀的医生。她比钟世藩小10岁，毕业于北京协和医学院的高级护理专业，曾在国立贵阳医学院（贵州医科大学的前身）工作。新中国成立后，廖月琴曾担任中山大学附属肿瘤医院副院长，她也是广东省肿瘤医院的创始人之一。

钟世藩与廖月琴在协和医学院读书时相识，于1934年结婚。二人婚后都在南京中央医院工作，两年后生下了长子钟南山。

1937年7月7日，日本制造"卢沟桥事变"，发动全面侵华战争，中国守军奋起抵抗。北平、天津相继失陷。1937年8月15日，日军开始轰炸南京。4个多月里，日军不分军事目标和民用目标，在南京上空肆意投弹空袭，给市民的生命财产造成了巨大损失。

在一次轰炸中，钟家的房屋被炸毁之时，尚在襁褓中的钟南山还在屋内。钟南山的母亲和外婆赶来，拼命地扒开一块块砖，最终从废墟下找到并救下了满脸是灰、命悬一线的钟南山。

1937年年底，南京中山医院撤退到贵阳，钟世藩带着妻儿也跟着搬到贵阳。他们在这里生活了8年，钟南山在这里度过了小学4年的时光。

1941年，廖月琴在贵阳生了一个女儿，钟世藩给女儿取名"钟黔君"。钟南山高兴极了，他有妹妹了。虽然战乱年代缺衣少食，但一家四口的生活非常温馨。

在钟南山的童年记忆里，经常有家长深夜带着孩子到他家里看病，钟世藩总是不厌其烦地为孩子们诊治。父亲的言传身教影响了钟南山，他从小就被医者救死扶伤、无私奉献的精神所感染。

第三章
调皮的男孩

在钟南山上小学三年级的时候,廖月琴给他一笔钱,让他交给学校当午餐费,钟南山却用这些钱去买了零食。廖月琴知道后,把这件事告诉了丈夫。钟南山以为父亲肯定要痛打他一顿,却没想到父亲不仅没动手,而且语气还极其平静。

钟世藩对儿子说:"南山,你好好想一想,你这么做到底对不对?"

钟南山听后十分惭愧。许多年以后他这样说:"爸爸这些话对我的刺激比他打我一顿更大。"

1945年,钟世藩又一次随医院举家搬迁

到广州。从此,一家人定居广州。

钟世藩在行医治病的同时还不忘搞科研。为了研究乙型脑炎病毒,他省吃俭用,用省下的钱买回三四百只小白鼠,在家里建起了实验室。老鼠的味道很大,那时候有人开玩笑说,如果要找钟世藩的家在哪里,顺着老鼠味找就行了。

在钟世藩做实验的时候,钟南山常好奇地在旁边观察。钟世藩看儿子对实验这么感兴趣,就让他帮忙饲养小白鼠,这也为钟南山日后从医打下了基础。

这时候的钟南山还不是很爱学习,倒是非常喜欢体育运动。从小学起他就常常参加各种体育比赛,并都取得了不错的成绩。但是他那时的学习成绩却差强人意,他还留过级,读了两次四年级。

钟南山在五年级的一次考试中偶尔取得

了不错的成绩。母亲廖月琴非常高兴，她对钟南山说："南山，你还是行的啊！"

钟南山听了，心灵上受到了很大的震撼。他后来说："那时我觉得妈妈一下子把我的一个亮点找出来了，我有了自尊心，觉得有人赞美我，从那时起我就开始认真读书了。"

看儿子学习这么努力，廖月琴鼓励他说，如果他能考上岭南大学附属中学，就奖励他一辆自行车。

男孩子谁不喜欢自行车呢？钟南山学习的劲儿更足了。1950年，钟南山小学毕业，考上了岭南大学附属中学。

廖月琴非常高兴。虽然当时战火刚停息，物资贫乏，通货膨胀，家里又很穷，但她还是给钟南山买了一辆自行车作为奖励。

钟南山在日记中记下："妈妈实现了她的诺言，给我买了一辆自行车，我是多么高兴啊。"

从那时起,钟南山就记住了一件事情:只要答应了别人的事情,就要做到。钟南山后来对自己、对孩子、对学生都是这么要求的,要么不答应,要么答应了就要做到。

第四章
重大的选择

在岭南大学附属中学读书时,钟南山的学习成绩始终名列前茅。初三毕业时,由于成绩优秀,钟南山直接升入了岭南大学附属中学的高中部。

钟南山不仅在学习上成绩优异,在体育上也展示出了过人的天赋。1955年,钟南山正在读高三,19岁的他参加了广东省田径比赛,取得了400米第二名的成绩,打破了当时广东省的纪录。之后,他又代表广东省参加了全国田径运动会,在400米比赛中,取得了全国第三名。

为此,他收到了中央体育学院(今北京

体育大学）的邀请，希望他到国家队参加培训。钟南山面临人生第一次重大选择：是成为一名专业运动员，还是参加高考？

钟南山与父亲商量时，钟世藩认为搞医学研究和治病救人是可以从事一生的事业，而运动员的体育生涯是有限的，所以希望他好好读书，将来做个医生。

钟南山经过慎重考虑，选择了放弃中央体育学院，报考北京医学院（今北京大学医学部）。北京医学院是中国顶级的医学院，是不少学子梦想中的高等学府。

1955年，钟南山以优异的成绩被北京医学院录取。当年广东省只有5名学生考上北京医学院，钟南山就是其中的一名。

刚进大学时，与来自全国各地的尖子生相比，钟南山的学习成绩并没那么出色，但钟南山是不会服输的。他奋起直追，经过努力，入学一年后，他不仅专业成绩优秀，田径成绩更是突飞猛进。

1956年，钟南山获得了北京市高校运动会的400米第一名，并当选为北京医学院三好学生，在人民大会堂接受了周恩来总理的接见。

1958年，大学三年级学生钟南山因为体育成绩出色，被选拔到北京市体育集训队，备战第一届中华人民共和国全国运动会，以非专业运动员的身份与全国职业高手同台对决。在第一届全运会比赛测验上，钟南山以54秒2的成绩打破了当时的400米栏的全国纪录。

运动会结束后，北京田径队希望钟南山加入。那时候专业运动员的待遇很不错，吃得也比一般人好，但钟南山拒绝了，他还是想当一名救死扶伤的医生。

第五章
甜蜜的婚姻

在北京读书的那段时间,钟南山经常去看望他的一位姨婆,他在姨婆家经常碰见一位叫李少芬的姑娘。原来李少芬的姑婆跟钟南山的姨婆是好朋友,一来二去,钟南山和李少芬因为上一辈人的友谊而相识。

李少芬是中国女篮的主力队员,钟南山也是个运动健将,两个年轻人很有共同话题。备战全运会时,钟南山经常去国家队的训练基地训练,正好中国女篮也在那里训练,于是钟南山和李少芬的见面机会就更多了。

两个年轻人慢慢熟悉起来,爱情的种子偷偷发芽,他们相爱了。

由于李少芬是国家队的队员，总是要出国比赛，两个人聚少离多。钟南山没有大男子主义思想，他对李少芬说："你就继续打吧，我愿意等。"

那时中国女篮在世界上已经很有名气了，有人开出了很高的薪水请李少芬去国外打球，但被李少芬拒绝了，一方面是为了国家，另一方面是因为钟南山还在等她。

李少芬后来回忆："法国人当时给我开出了很高的薪水，还许诺带我们一边打比赛一边周游世界。不过我不想去，一方面是我不想辜负培养了我的国家，一方面是那时我跟钟南山已经很要好了，所以更舍不得走。"

1963年12月31日，经历了八年爱情长跑的钟南山和李少芬在北京举行了简朴的婚礼。他们的新房不足10平方米，只摆得下一张床和简单的家具。

婚后，李少芬经常出去打比赛，钟南山作为医生工作也很繁忙，两个人聚少离多。虽然在一起的时间不多，但两个人的感情很好。

1966年，李少芬从国家队退役。当时她本可以留在国家队当教练，但她为了照顾身在广东的钟南山的父母和自己的母亲，毅然决定回到广东，任广东女篮教练。此时的钟南山还在北京工作，夫妻俩开始了两地分居的日子。

第六章
艰苦的岁月

1960年，钟南山从北京医学院大学毕业，留在学校的放射医学教研室工作。没过几年，"四清运动"开始了，正常的教学工作基本停滞了。

1964年，钟南山被下放到山东乳山，与当地农民同吃同住同劳动。山东农村的生活非常艰苦，但钟南山都坚持了下来。后来，当地村民深情回忆钟南山在当地生活工作的点点滴滴，很是感慨："给谁看病他都不要钱，这个人真了不起。"钟南山工作认真负责，农民们都对他赞不绝口。在下放期间，钟南山光荣地加入了中国共产党。

1966年，钟南山从山东回到了北京，这时"文化大革命"爆发了。钟南山的父亲钟世藩由于在国外留过学，被打成了"反动学术权威"。

受父亲的连累，钟南山被划成"走资派的狗崽子""反动学术权威的后代"，没能继续在学校从事临床医学工作，而是被安排去当了学校的锅炉工。一次学校组织献血，钟南山早上刚献完血，晚上还坚持烧锅炉，最终因为体力不支而晕倒在锅炉边。幸好来锅炉房打热水的人及时发现了他，挽救了他的生命。

1969年，北京医科大学派出了一支由114名师生组成的"新医药学教育革命探索队"到河北省的承德、宽城、平泉等地的农村、工厂下乡，钟南山就是这个队伍中的一员。在宽城的生活和工作条件异常艰苦，医疗队每天的工作就是做文艺宣传，真遇到病人时，却往往因为条件有限而难以救治，钟南山心里常为此而难过。

第七章
重回医疗领域

1971年,钟南山终于回到了广州,成为广州第四人民医院(今广州医学院第一附属医院)的一名医生。这时的他,已经35岁了。

有一天,父亲钟世藩问钟南山:"南山,你今年多少岁了?"

钟南山回答:"35岁。"

"35岁了,真可怕……"钟世藩叹了一口气,没再说什么。

要知道,钟世藩29岁时就已经在美国纽约州立大学拿到了博士学位,34岁时就当上了南京中央医院儿科主任。而35岁的钟南山,才刚刚走上医生的岗位,这怎么能不

让钟世藩感慨万千呢？

　　40多年后，钟南山回忆，一生中对他影响最大的一句话，就是父亲当年这句感叹。父亲的这句话深深刺激了钟南山，钟南山当时立下志愿，一定要在医学事业上奋力追赶，把逝去的时间抢回来！

　　虽然钟南山非常希望能当一名胸外科医生，但因为他在大学只学了3年半的医学知识，毕业后又整整11年都没有从事临床医疗工作，所以医院方面觉得他不适合当外科医生，给他安排到了内科门诊。

　　做了一段门诊大夫后，钟南山发现门诊接触到的病人有限，于是他主动请缨到急诊室去工作，没想到差点儿出了医疗事故。一天，钟南山随救护车到郊区接诊一个病人，当地卫生所说病人是肺结核大咯血，他想都没想就将其送往广州市结核病防治所。

第二天,当他走进急诊办公室时,主任严厉地对他说:"钟大夫,你昨天接的病人是消化道呕血,马上把他接回来。"

"咯血"和"呕血"是两个完全不同的概念,且出血的频度和色泽也不相同。还好病人被接回后通过手术死里逃生了,不过这次误诊却给了钟南山一个终身难忘的教训。

在接下来的时间里,钟南山拼命钻研医学知识,并做了4大本医疗工作笔记。8个月里他的体重整整掉了20斤,瘦得脱了相,不过他的医学事业有了跨越式的进步。他的医术已经比较熟练,成为合格的急诊医生,甚至达到了主治医生的水平。

第八章
迎难而上

1971年,国家号召全国医疗系统开展对呼吸科慢性支气管炎等呼吸疾病的防治研究。钟南山因临床诊断经验较少,就被分到了医院刚成立的"慢支炎防治小组"中。

当时没有人愿意研究慢性支气管炎这种治疗方法匮乏又难出成绩的病,钟南山心里也不太乐意,就去征求父亲钟世藩的意见。

钟世藩说:"捡难的事做,未必是坏事。"父亲的话犹如当头棒喝,钟南山下定了决心,服从组织安排。从此以后,他就开始专注于呼吸系统疾病的研究。

为了尽快成长为一个熟练的临床医生,

钟南山除了按时上班外，把大部分休息时间都用到X光室、心电图室、图书馆等地方。有的时候，他还会骑上自行车一个医院一个医院地去调查。

钟南山观察到，病人吐出的痰有黄的，有绿的，有泡沫状的，有黏稠状的，各不相同。有时候他在路上走着走着，就会突然蹲下来观察地上的痰。

那时候，钟南山经常和同事下乡采集农民痰液的标本。有一次钟南山在前面骑着单车，同事提心吊胆地抱着装着痰液样本的瓶子坐在后面的车座上。钟南山幽默地对同事说："你要拿好那个痰，要誓死保卫那个痰。"

经过多年的努力，钟南山逐步成长为中国顶尖的呼吸内科专家，他所在的科研小组也慢慢发展壮大。在1974年和1975年，小组在《中华医学杂志》和《中华内科杂志》

发表了两篇论文,打破了广州地区多年来没有论文在国家一级医学刊物发表的局面。

1978年,第一届全国科学大会在北京召开,钟南山与同事侯恕合写的论文《中西医结合分型诊断和治疗慢性气管炎》被评为国家科委全国科学大会成果一等奖。

1979年,"广州呼吸疾病研究所[①]"在钟南山所在的科研小组基础上成立,成为中国最早的呼吸疾病研究机构之一。

---

① 2017年8月,广州呼吸疾病研究所更名为"广州呼吸健康研究院"。

第九章
海外求学

1979年,钟南山考取了医院唯一的公派留学名额,远渡重洋到英国爱丁堡皇家医院学习两年,师从大卫·弗兰里教授。

弗兰里教授最初对这位年轻的中国医生并不信任。他向钟南山表示,他在爱丁堡皇家医院最多只能待8个月,而不是两年。

钟南山决定向导师证明自己。他把自己的研究方向确定为一氧化碳对血液氧气的影响,以便帮助弗兰里教授完成他的一个演算公式。

做实验需要有血液气体平衡仪,但是爱丁堡皇家医院的这台仪器坏掉了,购买新的

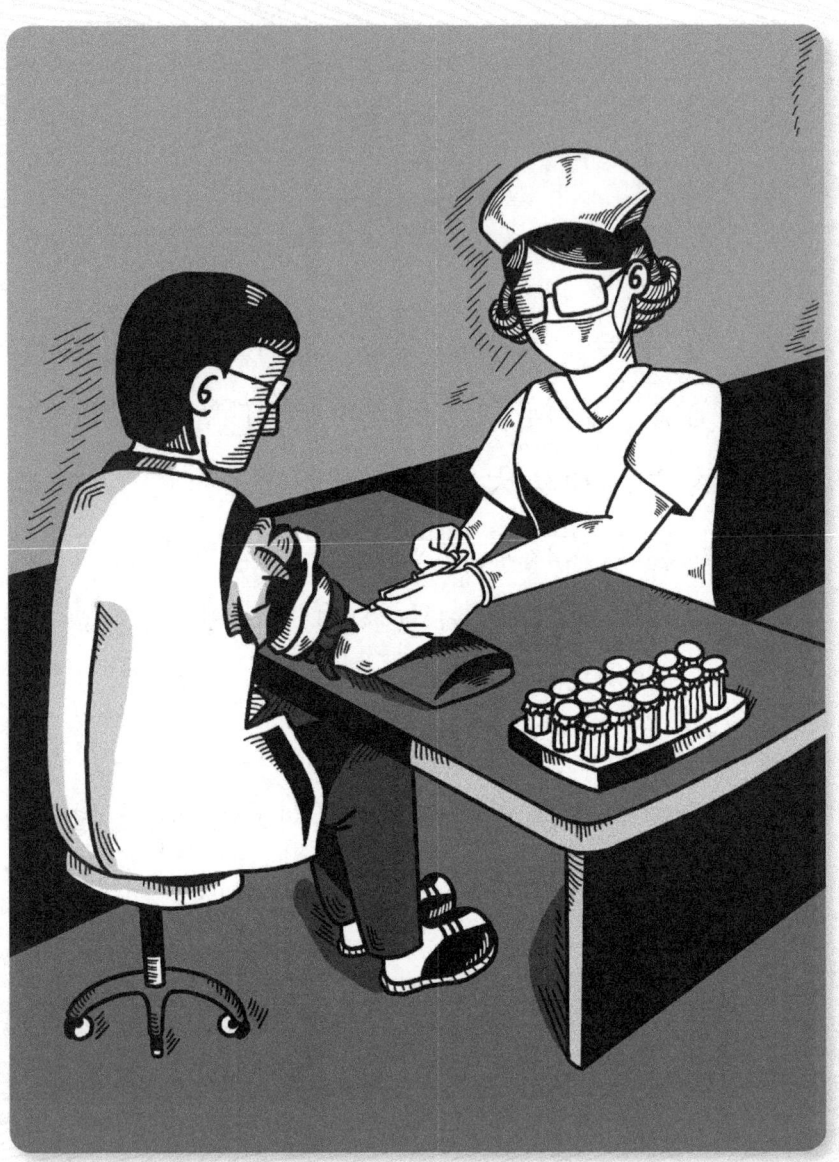

又需要时间。

钟南山等不及了,他决定自己动手维修机器。

为了检测仪器,钟南山先后从自己身上抽了800毫升的鲜血做实验。经过他的努力,终于让仪器恢复了正常运转。

这个研究是一氧化碳对血液氧气的影响,那么谁来做"小白鼠"呢?钟南山决定,他自己上!

钟南山一边吸入一氧化碳,一边让同事从自己身上抽血进行监测。

钟南山血液中的一氧化碳浓度直线上升,已经达到了15%,这相当于一个人连续吸食60支香烟后的浓度。

"太危险了!快停下来!"同行们惊叫。

钟南山虽感到天旋地转,头晕目眩,但为确保数据完整,他仍摇头坚持:"继续!"

他继续吸入一氧化碳,直到血液中的一氧化碳浓度达到22%!终于拿到了完整的数据。

这个实验不仅验证了弗兰里教授之前用数据推导方式得出的一氧化碳对血液氧气运输影响的推导公式,而且还发现推导公式不够完整。

弗兰里教授从此对这位中国学生刮目相看。"忘掉8个月吧,你爱干到什么时候都可以!"

留学两年间,钟南山取得了6项关于呼吸系统疾病防治研究的重要成果,完成了7篇学术论文,其中有4篇分别在英国医学研究学会、麻醉学会及糖尿病学会的期刊上发表。

弗兰里教授专门给中国驻英大使馆写信,表扬钟南山的成绩。他在信里说:"我从未遇到过一个学生像钟医生这样勤奋，合作得这样好，这么有成效。"

钟世藩知道后给钟南山写信，说："你终于用行动让外国人明白了，中国人不是一无是处。"

钟南山看到信后，流下了激动的泪水。在他的记忆里，他长这么大，这是父亲第一次表扬他。

以优异成绩毕业后，弗兰里教授力劝钟南山留在英国，并且说这里有三家医院、一家研究机构可以供他选择。

钟南山婉拒了导师的好意，他希望能够用自己的知识报效祖国。1981年11月18日，钟南山从伦敦飞回了祖国。

"在我心目中，好像从来没想过要留在那儿。国家在这么困难的时候给了我这样一个机会，有什么道理学了以后不回来？"钟南山后来在采访中这样说。

回国后，钟南山一直从事呼吸病学的诊治工作，历任广州呼吸疾病研究所所长、广州医学院院长、呼吸内科博士生导师，主持过多项国家攻关课题，获得多个国家级荣誉。

1987年，钟南山的父亲钟世藩去世，享年86岁。

钟世藩生前经常对钟南山说："一个人这辈子要在这个世界上留下一点儿东西，那么他这辈子就算没白活了。"

钟南山把这句话牢牢地记在心里，他继承父亲的遗志，在科研领域不断探索。

慢阻肺是"慢性阻塞性肺疾病"的简称，和糖尿病、冠心病、高血压一样，是四大慢性病之一，中国这种病的患者有1亿——占全球的三分之一。1989年，钟南山在中国首次提出了中国慢阻肺患者基础能耗校正公式。经过成百上千次试验，钟南山带领呼研所的科研人员研制出一种符合中国慢阻肺患者营养需求的全营养素——优特力生。

在支气管哮喘和气道高反应性的关系上，钟南山证实并发展了"隐匿型哮喘"的概念。1994年，他被联合国世界卫生组织聘为撰写《哮喘防治全球战略》文件的中国代表。

1996年，60岁的钟南山入选中国工程院院士，成为广东医药卫生界第一位中国工程院院士。

第十章
非典① 袭来

2002年年底,一种可怕的疾病在广东蔓延。这是一种人类历史上从未见过的传染病,如抢救不及时,病人很容易死于呼吸衰竭或多脏器衰竭。

2002年12月12日,钟南山所在的广州呼吸疾病研究所接收了一个奇怪的肺炎病人。这个病人的临床表现与典型肺炎不同,病人持续高热、干咳,肺部经X光透视呈现"白肺",使用各种抗生素毫不见效。

由于病人的肺部已经出现急性损伤,生

---

① "非典"是传染性非典型肺炎的中文简称,又称重症急性呼吸综合征(Severe Acute Respiratory Syndrome),英文简称SARS。

命垂危，于是钟南山试着用大剂量的皮质激素治疗，结果病人出现明显好转。

2003年1月2日，有消息传来，在广东省河源与这位病人有过接触的8个人都感染了与之前那个病例症状相同的肺炎。

钟南山非常吃惊。多年的行医经验告诉他，这是一例非常值得关注的特殊传染病。他马上向上级报告。随后，广东省中山市又爆发了多个相似病例。钟南山临危受命，和多位专家奔赴中山市对病人进行救治。

2003年1月22日，钟南山与多位专家一起将调查情况写成一份正式书面报告——《关于中山市不明原因肺炎调查报告》，正式将这一产生于广东的怪病命名为"非典型肺炎"，简称"非典"。《报告》写明了非典型肺炎的临床症状、治疗原则和预防措施，成为此后指导诊断、治疗非典型肺炎的重要依据。

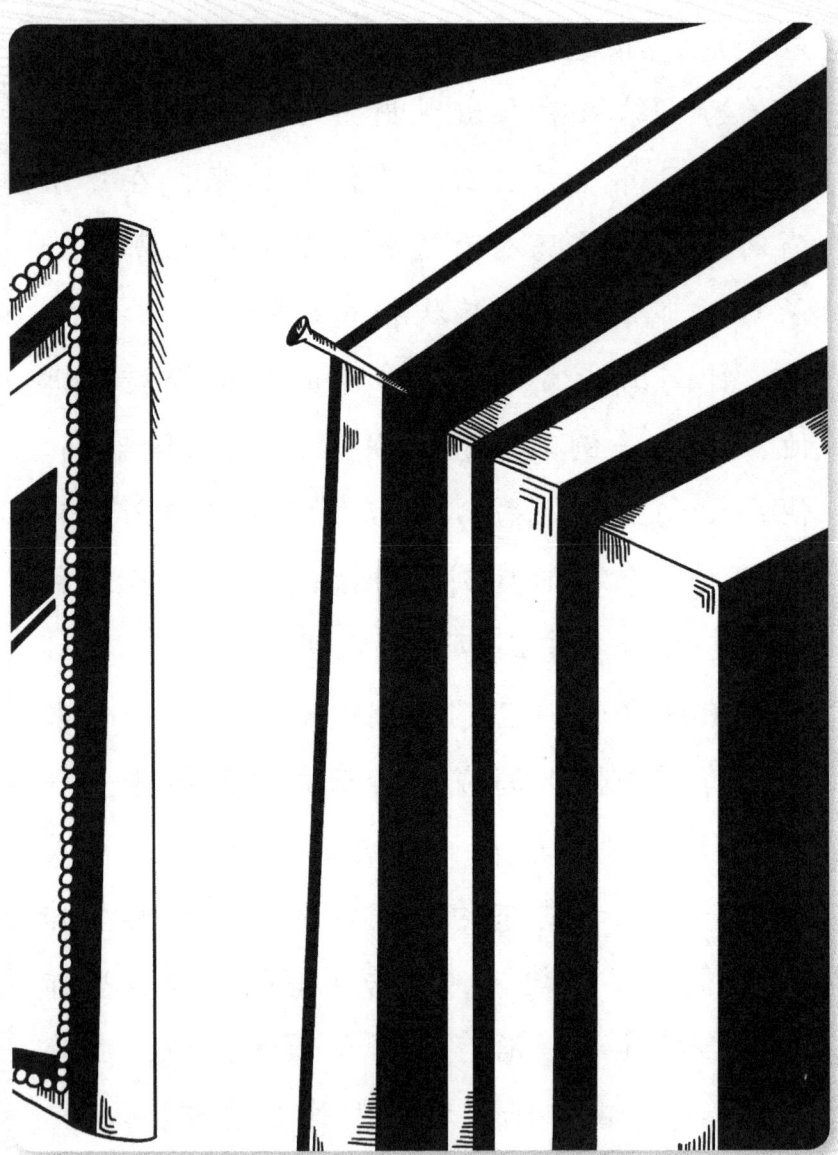

2003年2月18日，由于连续参加会诊、讲座及各种指导活动，连续38个小时没合眼的钟南山病倒了，出现了高烧、咳嗽和肺炎的症状，他只能停止工作，接受治疗。

出于稳定军心的考虑，钟南山没有选择在呼研所治疗，而是选择回到家中自我隔离治疗。他一边输液一边研究病历。家里没地方挂吊瓶，他就在门框上钉了一根大钉子，这根钉子至今没被拔掉。

钟南山事后说："那时候我还不知道自己能不能活，左胸很疼，很虚弱，拿个碗都会往下掉。但一直有个信念支撑着我，就是自己不能出事！"

钟南山养病的这段时间，妻子李少芬一直在他身边照顾他。她后来回忆说："他病的那几天，常常不想吃饭，体重下降得很厉害，我真的很着急。过去我当运动员，当体工队副大队长，东奔西跑，他帮我；现在，该我帮他了！"

所幸，钟南山得的不是"非典"，而是普通的肺炎。5天后拍片子，肺部的阴影消失了！病情刚刚好转，身体尚未恢复，钟南山便回到呼研所上班，抢救病人。

钟南山和他的研究团队日夜攻关，终于在短时间内摸索出了一套有效的救治办法，即"三早三合理"（早诊断、早隔离、早治疗；合理使用皮质激素、合理使用呼吸机、合理治疗并发症），在全世界率先形成了一套富有明显疗效的治疗方案。

这套方案大大提高了危重病人的成功抢救率，降低了死亡率，成为日后中国非典型肺炎诊治指南的基础，使得广东省非典型肺炎病死率全球最低（3.8%）、中国非典型肺炎的总体病死率位于国际上较低水平

（6.6%）。

到2003年3月，广东省累计报告"非典"病例已经突破了1000例。疫情在广东省蔓延，并向全国乃至全球扩散。考虑到广州呼吸研究所的技术力量，以及危重病人的较强传染性，钟南山主动向广东省卫生厅提出："把危重病人都送到我这里！"

这句话掷地有声，直到今天，人们依然能从这句话中感受到非凡的力量。虽然那时他已是67岁的老人，但是在疫情面前，他还像个骁勇善战的战士，毫不退缩。

第十一章
敢医敢言

在疫情早期,中国疾控中心的专家提出这次疫情的病原是衣原体,建议使用抗生素治疗。

衣原体是一种介于细菌和病毒之间的微生物,而衣原体感染的治疗方法和病毒感染的治疗方法是不相同的,如果方法错误,很有可能贻误治疗,加重患者的病情。

钟南山坐不住了,他公开反对病原体是衣原体的说法,坚持病原体可能是病毒。

钟南山事后说:"学术上的声音就是真理,就是事实。当我们看到这个学术的事实跟权威不一样时,我们当然首先尊重事实,而不是尊重权威……这不是一般的学术讨论，而是救命的问题。"

起初，对非典型性肺炎的报道并不多，直到2003年4月，中国的官方媒体对非典病例的报导才开始逐渐增多。

由于对这种疾病缺乏了解，谣言开始疯传，如"白醋可治疗肺炎"等，还引发了广州的白醋等物品的抢购潮，这股抢购潮伴随着谣言蔓延到了全国。

钟南山忧心如焚，他深知这场疫情正在全国范围内快速传播。如果不尽早公开信息，老百姓就不能采取正确的防疫措施，那么疫情只会愈演愈烈。

4月10日，北京召开了一场为世界卫生组织官员和中外记者举办的新闻发布会，钟南山被要求参加。第一天的会上，钟南山婉转的解释了当下的情况："作为专家，我觉得这个病可以控制，只要隔离得好就可以。"

第二天的会上，记者直接提问钟南山："那么按照你们的看法，是不是疫情已经得到了控制？"钟南山终于忍不住了："什么现在已经控制？根本就没有控制！"

整个会场一片哗然。钟南山继续说："目前还不能说是控制，只能说是遏制。控制的前提是要发现这个病源，同时找到对这个病源的处理方法。目前这个病的病源都还没搞清楚，怎么能说控制了？"

很快，关于此事的报道就得到了中央领导人的高度重视，总书记支持开展"国际大协作"。

4月16日，世界卫生组织正式宣布，SARS（重症急性呼吸综合征）的致病原为一种新的冠状病毒，并命名为SARS冠状病毒，证实了钟南山一直以来的看法。

4月20日国家卫生部部长、北京市委副书记由于防治"非典"不力被免职。这一天被外界称为"改写中国抗击非典的里程碑"。

钟南山的坚持，使得中国抗击非典的战役发生了里程碑式的变化。4月21日，卫生部建立每日疫情发布制度。两天后（4月23日），国务院成立防治SARS指挥部，统一指挥、协调全国SARS的防治工作。此后，抗击SARS工作走上正轨。

7月2日，广医一院最后三名非典病人康复出院，中国抗击非典疫情成功。钟南山和他的团队连续工作193天，收治病例302例，不仅创下非典时期最长工作时间记录，还取得了出院率93%的成绩。

2003年7月13日，全球不再增加新增病例和疑似病例，疫情基本结束。

在抗击非典斗争中，钟南山始终战斗在

最前列，为取得抗疫胜利做出了重要贡献，赢得了全国人民的爱戴和敬仰。全国劳动模范、全国优秀共产党员、全国卫生系统抗击非典先进个人、全国白求恩奖章、广东省模范共产党员、广东省医德医风标兵、广东省抗击非典特等功、广州市抗击非典先进个人、广东省科技特等奖励……面对如潮水一样涌来的鲜花和荣誉，钟南山始终保持谦虚的态度。他多次说："其实，我不过就是一个看病的大夫。"

2004年2月20日，由中央电视台举办的"感动中国2003年度人物评选"落下帷幕，钟南山以高票当选。给钟南山的颁奖词是这样的："面对突如其来的SARS疫情，他冷静、无畏，他以医者的妙手仁心挽救生命，以科学家实事求是的科学态度应对灾难。他说，'在我们这个岗位上，做好防治疾病的工作,就是最大的政治'。这掷地有声的话语,表现出他的人生准则和职业操守。他以令人敬仰的学术勇气、高尚的医德和深入的科学探索给予了人们战胜疫情的力量。"

第十二章
不断进步

"非典"过后,钟南山仍坚守在临床一线,门诊、会诊、查房一样不落。此外,在专业科研领域他也一刻没有放松。他先后主持中国国内及WHO/GOLD委员会全球协作课题等重大课题10余项,并在国际权威学术期刊上发表SCI论文540余篇,在中华医学会等机构主办的国家级杂志上发表论文400余篇,出版各类专著20余部,获发明专利近60项,实用新型30余项。

"再好的东西,如果没法在社会上广泛应用,就没有走完创新的过程。"钟南山说。他认为,做科研既要"顶天"也要"立地"。"顶天"就是要抓住国际前沿理念、攻关国家急需的项目,"立地"就是要能解决老百姓的需求,研发出老百姓欢迎的有效、安全、价廉、方便的器械和药物。

钟南山率领团队打造了呼吸疾病国家重点实验室产学研体系,研发适合中国国情的药物及早期防治新战略。钟南山和他的团队发现,一种常用的廉价国产祛痰药物羧甲司坦可显著减少慢阻肺的急性发作达24.5%,慢阻肺常规治疗费也可减少85%。这篇论文名为《羧甲司坦对慢性阻塞性肺疾病急性发作的作用(PEACE研究):一项随机安慰剂对照研究》,2008年6月在世界顶级医学杂志《柳叶刀》上发表,并被《柳叶刀》评选为"2008年度论文",这是中国科研工作者首次获得这一殊荣。

2009年6月,广东珠三角进入了甲型流

感暴发期，各地陆续出现甲流患者；2013年3月，沪皖两地发现H7N9新型禽流感，随后全国各地陆续上报新型禽流感病例……在这两次新型突发呼吸道传染病中，钟南山都带领他的团队发挥了至关重要的作用。

多年来，钟南山坚守在抗击疫情第一线，还带领团队探索建立符合中国国情的呼吸道重大传染病防控体系，建立了国际先进的新发特发呼吸道重大传染病"防—治—控"医疗周期链式管理体系，为推动中国建立公共卫生防治体系、提高重大疫情侦查监测能力和效率、加强应急队伍建设等方面发挥了重要作用。

他还主动承担起突发公共卫生事件代言人的角色，发表大量呼吸系统疾病科普文章，在无数场直播、专题栏目、讲座中呼吁公众关注呼吸道健康，努力让公众穿上医学知识

的盔甲。

2018年12月18日,党中央、国务院授予钟南山"改革先锋"称号,颁授"改革先锋"奖章,并称钟南山为"公共卫生事件应急体系建设的重要推动者"。

第十三章
再战新冠

2019年12月,湖北省武汉市部分医院陆续发现了多例有华南海鲜市场暴露史的不明原因肺炎病例。病人出现的前期症状和流感比较相似,都是会出现全身乏力并且咳嗽。

12月26日,湖北省中西医结合医院医生张继先在接诊时发现,发热不是这种新型肺炎的必要表现。不少人并无发热,只是干咳,肺部却有显著病变。她将此种病例向医院做了汇报,医院27日立即上报给江汉区疾控中心。29日,湖北和武汉卫健委指示相关疾控中心和医院开展流行病学研究。

随着武汉市病例的逐渐增多,疫情开始

引发全国关注。84岁的钟南山教授再次临危受命，出任国家卫健委高级别专家组组长。

2020年1月8日，国家卫健委专家组初步确认新型冠状病毒为疫情病源。

1月11日，中国疾控中心将整条新冠病毒全基因组序列上传网站，同全球和世卫组织共享数据。

武汉的疫情牵动着全中国人民的心。这次的疫情是不是SARS？源头在哪儿？是否存在人传人的现象？人们迫切想听到权威的声音。这个权威就是钟南山。

记者采访时，他给公众的建议是："我总的看法，就是没有特殊的情况，不要去武汉。"

但1月18日傍晚，他还是义无反顾地赶往武汉防疫最前线。由于正值春运，当天飞机票已经卖完，而高铁票也已经没有座位了，最后他被安排在高铁的餐车座位上。

钟南山抵达武汉当夜便迅速赶往武汉市卫生健康委员会了解情况，连夜开展工作。

1月19日上午，钟南山先参加疫情研讨会听武汉疾控中心和卫健委通报疫情，再迅速前往集中收治患者的武汉市金银潭医院和武汉疾控中心实地调研。中午他来不及休息，与各位专家开会到下午5点，之后又登上了飞往北京的航班。晚上10点到达北京后，他马上赶往国家卫健委开会。会议结束回到酒店，已是第二天的凌晨2点。

1月20日，钟南山在答记者问时证实了新冠病毒"人传人"的事实。他提醒：普通人要提高警惕，没有特殊情况不要去武汉；有类似感冒的症状要及时到发热门诊就诊；出门要记得戴口罩，买不到N95，普通口罩也可以起到阻止飞沫传播的作用；源头目前不清楚，但可能是竹鼠、獾这类野生动物，尽量别去碰野味……人们这才意识到这种病毒的严重性。随后，各个省份陆续启动一级响应，抗击新型冠状病毒肺炎疫情的战役在中国打响。

1月21日，科技部组织召开"新型冠状病毒联防联控工作机制科研攻关组第一次会议"。会议宣布成立以钟南山院士为组长、由14位专家组成的新型冠状病毒感染的肺炎疫情联防联控工作机制科研攻关专家组。此后，钟南山带领团队马不停蹄，一边进行临床救治，一边开展科研攻关。

2月13日，钟南山团队宣布从新冠肺炎患者的粪便样本中分离出新冠病毒。

2月14日，在钟南山指导下，呼吸疾病国家重点实验室联合中科院广州生物医药与健康研究院等研发出新冠病毒IgM抗体快速检测试剂盒。

2月28日，钟南山与全国30多位作者共同完成"中国2019年新型冠状病毒感染的临床特征"研究，并在国际医学期刊《新英格兰医学杂志》发表。该研究收集了来自中国552家医院的1099例确诊患者的临床信息，提出严格、及时地采取流行病学措施，对遏制疫情迅速蔓延至关重要。

钟南山还多次通过远程医疗平台为湖北等地危重症患者会诊，给当地医生和患者吃下"定心丸"。在与前方进行病例探讨时，钟南山强调，不管是多么危重的病人，都要全力救治，绝不放弃。

目前新冠疫情在中国已经得到有效控制，但全球其他国家的疫情却依然严峻。钟南山始终坚守在国际医学研究一线，第一时间分享中国的抗疫经验。

"传染病是没有国界的。只要有一个国

家不做干预，全球新冠疫情就不会消失。"钟南山说。

钟南山先后和多个国家的医学专家及驻华使团代表进行视频连线，从隔离措施、病例数据、治疗方法等多个方面分享经验，为全球共同抗击疫情积极贡献力量。

"通过交流，可让其他国家少走弯路。"钟南山说，"因为我们走过了艰难的路，所以要相互支持。"

2020年年底，受境外输入的影响，中国国内疫情又有所抬头。2021年1月25日，85岁的钟南山院士在微信公众号上发布了一段25秒的视频，寥寥数语，却感人至深。他在视频中说："春节是中国人骨子里的情结，但是今年春节却有千千万万的人选择留下。为防疫'牺牲'团圆，每个人都了不起。我是钟南山，我在广州，谢谢过年不回家的你。"

Chapter One

Winner of the Medal of the Republic

On the morning of September 8, 2020, a solemn meeting was held in the Great Hall of the People in Beijing to commend and reward those outstanding individuals and groups who had made tremendous contributions to China's fight against the COVID-19 epidemic.

A vibrant, 84-year-old man stepped up to the stage to accept the award. He is Zhong Nanshan, and he is the winner of the Medal of the Republic, China's highest honor awarded to those outstanding figures for their tremendous contributions to the country.

When President Xi Jinping conferred the medal on Zhong Nanshan, the audience burst into prolonged applause.

But who is Zhong Nanshan? And why was he awarded this special honor?

Zhong Nanshan is an academician of the Chinese Academy of Engineering and director of the National Clinical Research Center for Respiratory Disease of the First Affiliated Hospital of Guangzhou Medical University. After the outbreak of the COVID-19 epidemic, he gave honest and accurate information to the public about the disease, presented his "human-to-human transmission" conclusion in a timely manner. He emphasized strict prevention and control measures, led his team in drawing up the diagnosis and treatment protocol for COVID-19, and made outstanding contributions to epidemic response, treatment of critical cases, and scientific research.

After receiving the medal, he said, "'Health entrusted, and lives confided.' This has always been my original aspiration, and protecting the health and lives of the people has always been my mission as a doctor."

He also battled the severe acute respiratory syndrome (SARS) in 2003. During that time and while fighting the COVID-19 epidemic, Zhong Nanshan has taken practical actions to fulfill his original aspiration and mission, earning him the respect and admiration of the Chinese people.

Chapter Two

The Eldest Son of the Zhong Family

Zhong Nanshan was born on October 20, 1936 in Nanjing Central Hospital. Because the hospital was located to the south of Zhongshan Mountain in Nanjing, his father Zhong Shifan named him "Nanshan" (meaning south mountain in Chinese).

Zhong Shifan, Zhong Nanshan's father, was born in 1901. He was raised by his uncle after his parents died young. He studied hard even though he had to work for a living at the same time, and was finally admitted to Peking Union Medical College with excellent grades. Upon graduation, he went to study at the State University of New York in the United States, and received a doctorate in medicine in 1930. Over the years he served as director of the Pediatrics Departments of Nanjing and Guiyang Central

Hospitals, professor of the Pediatrics Department of Xiangya Medical College, director of Guangzhou Central Hospital and its Pediatrics Department, professor and director of the Pediatrics Department of Lingnan University School of Medicine, and professor and director of the Pediatrics Department of Sun Yat-sen University Zhongshan School of Medicine in Guangzhou.

Liao Yueqin, Zhong Nanshan's mother, was also an excellent doctor. She was 10 years younger than Zhong Shifan. She graduated from Peking Union Medical College with a major in advanced nursing and later worked at the National Guiyang Medical College (predecessor of Guizhou Medical University). After the founding of the People's Republic of China in 1949, she served as deputy dean of the Sun Yat-sen University Affiliated Cancer Hospital. She was also one of the founders of Guangdong Cancer Hospital.

Zhong Shifan and Liao Yueqin met each other when they were studying at Peking Union Medical College. They were married in 1934, and afterwards both worked at Nanjing Central Hospital. Two years later, they gave birth to Zhong Nanshan, their eldest son.

On July 7, 1937, Japan engineered the "Lugouqiao Incident" and launched a full-scale war of aggression against China. The Chinese defenders rose in resistance against the Japanese invaders. Beijing and Tianjin fell one after another. On August 15, 1937, Japan began bombing Nanjing. For over four months, the Japanese invaders arbitrarily bombed and launched air strikes on both military and civilian targets, causing huge losses of life and catastrophic destruction.

While just an infant, Zhong Nanshan was still in when their house was bombed. His mother and grandmother rushed back, desperately dug through the rubble and bricks, and finally found and rescued the infant whose face was covered with dust and whose life was hanging by a thread.

At the end of 1937, Nanjing Central Hospital was relocated to Guiyang, and Zhong Shifan moved there with his wife and son. They lived there for eight years, and Zhong Nanshan spent four years studying in a primary school there.

In 1941, Liao Yueqin gave birth to a daughter, and Zhong Shifan named his daughter Zhong Qianjun. Zhong Nanshan was very happy to have a younger sister. Despite the lack of food and clothing during the war, their family was living a happy life.

Zhong Nanshan remembers that during these days, people often took their sick children to his home late at night to seek medical treatment from his father, and Zhong Shifan never turned anyone away. With his father as an example, the young Zhong Nanshan experienced firsthand the selfless dedication of doctors who healed the wounded and saved the dying.

Chapter Three

A Naughty Boy

When Zhong Nanshan was in the third grade, Liao Yueqin gave him some money to pay for his school lunch, but he used it to buy snacks instead. Liao Yueqin told her husband about this. Zhong Nanshan was certain he'd receive a good beating from his father, and did not expect what would happen next.

His father sat and talked with him in a very calm tone, saying to his son, "Nanshan, think about what you did. Was it the right thing to do?"

Zhong Nanshan was very ashamed. Many years later, he said, "My father's words got to me harder than an actual beating."

In 1945, the family moved once again, this time to Guangzhou. It was here that they finally settled down.

In addition to medical practice, Zhong Shifan was active in scientific research. He saved money to set up a small home laboratory to study the Encephalitis B virus. He bought three to four hundred mice which smelled very foul. At that time, people joked that if you wanted to find Zhong Shifan's home, just follow the smell of mice.

Zhong Nanshan curiously watched his father as he conducted the experiments. Seeing his son show a keen interest in the research, Zhong Shifan asked if he'd like to help raise the mice, which he knew would help prepare him to become a doctor in the future.

At that time, Zhong Nanshan was not very fond of studying, and he was into sports. Though he was very good in sports during primary school, his academic record was not good. He also failed to advance to the next grade and had to repeat the fourth grade.

In the fifth grade he achieved a high score on an exam. His mother was so happy that she said to him, "Nanshan, you can get high score!"

This greatly inspired him. He later said, "At that time, I felt that my mother had recognized my merit. She had praised me, which helped me regain self-esteem. From that time on, I started to study conscientiously."

Seeing her son study so hard, Liao Yueqin encouraged him by telling him that if he could be admitted to the Affiliated Middle School of Lingnan University, she would reward him with a bicycle.

As all boys like bicycles, Zhong Nanshan studied even harder. In 1950, he graduated from primary school and was admitted to the Affiliated Middle School of Lingnan University.

His mother was overjoyed. Although the war had recently ended, goods were still in short supply. There was inflation, and the family was poor. Despite all this, she was still able to buy a bicycle as a reward.

Zhong Nanshan wrote in his diary, "My mother kept her promise and bought me a bicycle. I'm so happy."

This event impressed upon him an important lesson: if he makes a promise, he must fulfill it. He would apply this ideal to himself throughout his life, and later teach it to his children and students. He would either refuse to agree to do something, or be certain to do it if he agreed.

Chapter Four

A Crucial Choice

Zhong Nanshan's academic record was among the top percentile at the Affiliated Middle School of Lingnan University. When he graduated from the third grade of the junior high school, he advanced directly to the senior high school because of his excellent marks.

Zhong Nanshan not only had an excellent academic record, but he also demonstrated extraordinary talent in sports. In 1955, he was in the third year of the senior high school. At the age of 19, he participated in the Guangdong Provincial Track and Field Competition and won second place in the 400-meter race, breaking the record of Guangdong Province at that time. Later, on behalf of Guangdong Province, he participated in the National Athletics Games and ranked third in the 400-meter race.

For this reason, he received an offer from the Central Sport Institute (present-day Beijing Sport University) to train for the national team. This was the first crucial choice of his life: to become a professional athlete or take the national college entrance examination.

Zhong Nanshan asked for his father's opinion. His father told him that medical research and curing diseases to save patients could be a lifelong career, but an athlete's sports career was limited. He hoped that his son would study hard and become a doctor in the future.

After careful consideration, Zhong Nanshan chose to decline the Central Sport Institute and apply to Beijing Medical College (present-day Peking University Health Science Center). At that time, Beijing Medical College was the top medical school in the country, and an institution of higher learning that many students dreamt of attending. It still holds that prestigious reputation today.

In 1955, he was admitted to Beijing Medical College with excellent grades, one of the five students from Guangdong Province admitted that year.

At first, his academic performance was not as good as other top students from around the country. But he did not admit defeat. He tried his best to catch up. He studied hard, and a year later he was getting excellent marks and had also made great progress in track and field.

In 1956, he won first place in the 400-meter race in the Beijing University Games, and was elected as the "Triple-A Student" in terms of moral integrity, academic records and sports of Beijing Medical College. He was received by Premier Zhou Enlai in the Great Hall of the People.

In 1958, as a third-year college student, he was selected to join the Beijing Sports Training Team to prepare for the First National Games of the People's Republic of China. At the games, he competed against professional athletes from all over the country. As a non-professional athlete, Zhong Nanshan broke the national record of the 400-meter hurdle with a time of 54.2 seconds in a trial race of the First National Games.

After this outstanding performance at the First National Games, the Beijing Track and Field Team hoped that Zhong Nanshan would join them. At that time, professional athletes received preferential treatment, and their diet was better, but Zhong Nanshan refused. He still wanted to be a doctor who heals the wounded and saves the dying.

Chapter Five

A Sweet Marriage

While studying in Beijing, Zhong Nanshan often visited his great-aunt. At her place, he often met a girl named Li Shaofen whose great-aunt was a close friend of Zhong's great-aunt. Zhong Nanshan and Li Shaofen came to know each other because of the friendship of the older generation.

Li Shaofen was a key player on the Chinese women's basketball team, and Zhong Nanshan was also an excellent athlete. In sports, the two young people shared a common passion. Zhong Nanshan would often go to the national training camp to prepare for the First National Games, which was also where the Chinese women's basketball team trained. They would often have opportunities to meet each other.

Over time they gradually got to know better of each other, and the seeds of love began to sprout.

Since Li Shaofen was on the Chinese women's basketball team, she always had to travel for competitions, making it difficult for them to get together. Zhong Nanshan did not mind this, telling her, "You can continue to play basketball. I am willing to wait."

At that time, the Chinese women's basketball team was already very famous in the world. In fact, Li Shaofen was offered the opportunity to go abroad to play basketball with a high salary, but she refused because she wanted to play for her country and Zhong Nanshan was still waiting for her.

Li Shaofen later recalled, "The French offered me a very high salary to play basketball, which would also allow me to travel around the world. But I didn't want to go abroad. For one thing, I wanted to remain loyal to the country that nurtured me. Also at that time, Zhong Nanshan and I were in a serious relationship, and I was very reluctant to leave him."

After being together for eight years, Zhong Nanshan and Li Shaofen held a simple wedding in Beijing on December 31, 1963. Their new apartment was less than 10 square meters, with only a bed and some simple furniture.

Li Shaofen would often go on tours to play basketball while Zhong Nanshan was very busy working as a doctor. Although they did not have much time to be together, their love was deep.

In 1966, Li Shaofen retired from the Chinese women's basketball team. At that time, she could have worked as a coach for the team, but she decided instead to go to Guangdong where she could take care of her mother and Zhong Nanshan's parents. There, she also worked as a coach for the

Guangdong women's basketball team. Meanwhile, Zhong Nanshan was still working in Beijing. The couple had to live apart.

Chapter Six

Hard Years

In 1960, Zhong Nanshan graduated from Beijing Medical College and worked in its radiological medicine teaching and research section. A couple years later, the "four clean-ups" movement (a movement aimed at cleaning things up in the political, economic, organizational and ideological fields from 1963-1966) began. Normal teaching basically stagnated.

In 1964, Zhong Nanshan was sent to Rushan, Shandong Province where he ate, lived and labored with local farmers. Life in the rural areas of Shandong was very hard, but Zhong Nanshan endured it. Local villagers later recalled details of Zhong Nanshan's life and work there, saying emotionally, "He cured diseases free of charge.

He was really remarkable." Zhong Nanshan was conscientious and responsible for his work, and all the farmers spoke highly of him. While living and working there, he became a member of the Communist Party of China (CPC).

When the Cultural Revolution started in 1966, Zhong Nanshan returned to Beijing. His father had been labeled a "reactionary academic authority" because he had studied abroad.

Because of his father, Zhong Nanshan was stigmatized as "a son of the capitalist-roader" (a political label often pinned on cadres by the Red Guards during the Cultural Revolution) and "a descendant of reactionary academic authority". He was unable to continue his clinical medical work and was instead assigned to work in the boiler room at the college. One time, he had just finished donating blood during a school blood drive in the morning and had returned to work in the boiler room. At some point, he fainted by the boiler from exhaustion. Fortunately, someone who came to the boiler room to get hot water that evening found him in time and saved his life.

In 1969, Beijing Medical College sent a "new medicine education revolutionary exploration team" composed of 114 teachers and students to the rural areas and factories in Chengde, Kuancheng, and Pingquan, Hebei Province. Zhong Nanshan was one of them. The living and working conditions in Kuancheng were extremely poor. The medical team's daily work was to promote art and literature. When he had patients, it was often difficult to cure them because of limited medical resources. He felt very sad about this.

Chapter Seven

Serving as a Doctor Again

In 1971, Zhong Nanshan finally returned to Guangzhou where he became a doctor at the Fourth People's Hospital of Guangzhou (present-day First Affiliated Hospital of Guangzhou Medical University). He was 35 years old.

One day, his father asked him, "Nanshan, how old are you this year?"

Zhong Nanshan replied, "I'm 35."

His father shook his head and sighed. "35 years old, it's terrible...."

When his father was 29 years old, he had received a doctorate from the State University of New York, and by the time he was 34 he had become director of the Pediatrics Department of Nanjing Central Hospital. Here was his son, a 35-year-old man, who had only just become a doctor.

Over 40 years later, Zhong Nanshan would recall that the words that have influenced him most in his life were those said by his father while sighing. It affected him deeply. He recalled that it motivated him to work harder to compensate for the lost time.

Although Zhong Nanshan had hoped to be a thoracic surgeon, he only studied for three and a half years. Upon graduation, he had not been engaged in clinical work for 11 years, so the hospital thought that he was not fit to be a surgeon. He was assigned to the outpatient department of internal medicine.

Through working as an outpatient doctor, he had a limited number of patients through the outpatient service. He volunteered to work in the emergency department. One time, however, he almost caused a medical accident unexpectedly. He went to the suburbs with an ambulance one day to pick up a patient. The local clinic said that the patient had tuberculosis with severe hemoptysis. Zhong Nanshan took the patient to Guangzhou Tuberculosis Prevention and Control Center without even thinking about it.

When he walked into the emergency office the next day, the director sternly said to him, "Dr. Zhong, the patient you received yesterday has suffered from hematemesis in the digestive tract. Bring him here immediately."

"Hemoptysis" and "hematemesis" are two different concepts, and the frequency and color of bleeding also vary. The patient was brought to the hospital and underwent an emergency operation. Fortunately, he was saved. However, this misdiagnosis taught

Zhong Nanshan an unforgettable lesson.

After that, he devoted his free time to self-study, and even filled four notebooks full of medical notes. He studied so much that sometimes he would not even eat, and in eight months he lost 10 kilograms. As a result, however, his medical career experienced a great leap forward. He'd become more medically proficient and soon became a qualified emergency doctor, even reaching the level of attending doctor.

Chapter Eight

Rising to the Challenge

In 1971, the state called on the national medical system to carry out research on the prevention and treatment of respiratory diseases such as chronic bronchitis in the Respiratory Department. Zhong Nanshan was assigned to the newly established Chronic Bronchitis Prevention and Treatment Team in the hospital because he had little experience in clinical diagnosis.

At that time, no one was willing to study chronic bronchitis, a disease that lacked therapies and was difficult to achieve research results. Zhong Nanshan was not happy with this assignment, so he went to ask his father for advice.

"It is not necessarily a bad thing to do a difficult

thing," his father replied. His words brought Zhong Nanshan to his senses, so he made up his mind to obey the hospital's work assignments. From then on, he focused on researching respiratory diseases.

In addition to his normal work tasks, Zhong Nanshan spent most of his remaining time in the X-ray room, electrocardiogram room and library, hoping to become a skilled clinician as soon as possible. Sometimes he would ride his bicycle to different hospitals to conduct additional research.

He observed that the sputum spit out by patients was different. It can be yellow, green, foamy, or viscous. Sometimes while walking on the road, he would suddenly squat and observe sputum on the ground.

During this time, Zhong Nanshan and his colleague would often go to the countryside to collect sputum samples from farmers. One day they were riding a bicycle, with his colleague sitting behind him and fearfully holding a bottle of sputum sample. Zhong Nanshan humorously told his colleague, "You must take good care of the sample and guard it with your life!"

After years of hard work, Zhong Nanshan gradually became China's top expert on respiratory internal medicine, and his scientific research team continued to grow. In 1974 and 1975, the team published two papers in the *National Medical Journal of China* and the *Chinese Journal of Internal Medicine*, the first time in many years that papers from Guangzhou had been published in national first-level medical journals.

In 1978, the First National Science Conference was held in Beijing. Zhong Nanshan's paper entitled "Diagnosis and Treatment of Chronic Bronchitis by Integrated Traditional Chinese and Western Medicine," which he co-authored with his colleague

Hou Shu, won first prize for research results, awarded by the State Scientific and Technological Commission.

In 1979, the Guangzhou Institute of Respiratory Diseases (renamed the Guangzhou Institute of Respiratory Health in August 2017) was established on the basis of Zhong Nanshan's research team and became one of the earliest respiratory disease research institutions in China.

Chapter Nine
Studying Abroad

In 1979, Zhong Nanshan excelled in the exam to receive the hospital's scholarship to study abroad. This enabled him to travel to Edinburgh, Scotland where he studied at the Royal Infirmary of Edinburgh for two years under the tutelage of Professor David Franley.

Professor Franley initially did not trust the young Chinese doctor. He told Zhong Nanshan that he could only stay at the Royal Infirmary of Edinburg for eight months at most, instead of two years.

Zhong Nanshan was determined to prove himself to his supervisor. He chose for his research direction the effects of carbon monoxide on blood oxygen, so as to help Professor Franley complete one of his experiments.

The experiment required a blood-gas balance instrument, but the instrument at the Royal Infirmary of Edinburg had broken, and it would take time to buy a new one.

Zhong Nanshan couldn't wait, so he decided to repair the instrument himself.

To test it after his repair, he drew blood from his own body. After drawing altogether 800 ml blood from Zhong Nanshan at different tests, the instrument began to operate normally.

The research focused on the effects of carbon monoxide on blood oxygen, so who would become the "lab mouse"? Again, Zhong Nanshan decided to do it himself.

While inhaling carbon monoxide, he asked

his colleague to draw blood from his body for monitoring.

The concentration of carbon monoxide in his blood rose sharply and reached 15 percent, which was equivalent to the level after a person smoked 60 cigarettes.

"It's too dangerous! Stop this!" his colleagues exclaimed.

Although he felt dizzy, he shook his head. He wanted to ensure they could capture a complete data sample. "Continue," he told his colleagues.

He continued to inhale the carbon monoxide until the concentration in his blood reached 22 percent. Finally, he got all the data.

The experiment not only confirmed certain aspects of Professor Franley's derivation formula on the effects of carbon monoxide on blood oxygen transport, but also proved that his formula was incomplete.

Professor Franley was impressed by the Chinese student. "Forget about eight months. You can study here as long as you like."

During his two years of studying abroad, Zhong Nanshan achieved six important research results on the prevention and treatment of respiratory diseases and completed seven academic papers, four of which were published in the journals of the British Medical Research Council, the Anesthesiology Society and the Diabetes Society.

Professor Franley wrote to the Chinese Embassy in the UK to commend Zhong Nanshan's achievements. He said in the letter, "I have never met a student who is as diligent as Dr. Zhong, cooperates so well, and is so effective."

After his father learned about this, he wrote to Zhong Nanshan, "With your actions you have made foreigners finally understand that Chinese people are not worthless."

After Zhong Nanshan read the letter, he was tearful. It was the first time that he could remember his father ever praising him.

Upon his graduation with honors, Professor Franley asked Zhong Nanshan to stay in the UK, telling him there were three hospitals and one research institute from which he could choose to work.

Zhong Nanshan declined the kindness of his supervisor as he'd wanted to use his knowledge to serve his motherland. On November 18, 1981, he flew back to China from London.

He later said in an interview, "As I recall, I never really considered staying there. My country had given me such a great opportunity during such a difficult time. There was no reason for me not to come back after studying abroad."

After returning to China, he was engaged in the diagnosis and treatment of respiratory diseases. He served as director of the Guangzhou Institute of Respiratory Diseases, dean of the Guangzhou Medical College, and the doctoral supervisor of respiratory internal medicine. He also took charge of a few key national research projects and won a few national honorary titles.

In 1987, his father died at the age of 86.

During his lifetime, his father had often told him, "If a person wants to leave something in this world behind, then he will not idle his life away."

Zhong Nanshan had always kept these words in mind. He took on his father's mantle, and continued his explorations in scientific research.

COPD is the acronym for chronic obstructive pulmonary disease. It is one of the four chronic diseases along with diabetes, coronary heart disease, and hypertension. There are 100 million patients affected with COPD in China — one-third of the world's total. In 1989, Zhong Nanshan first proposed the basic energy consumption correction formula for Chinese COPD patients in China. After many experiments, he led research team of the Guangzhou Institute of Respiratory Diseases to develop Nutrient—a complete nutrient that meets the nutritional needs of Chinese COPD patients.

On the relationship between bronchial asthma and airway hyperreactivity, Zhong Nanshan developed and refined the definition of asymptomtic asthma. In 1994, he authored part of Global Strategy for Asthma Management and Prevention published by the World Health Organization.

In 1996, 60-year-old Zhong Nanshan was elected as an academician of the Chinese Academy of Engineering and became the first academician majoring in medicine and health from Guangdong.

Chapter Ten

Fighting SARS

At the end of 2002, a terrible disease spread in Guangdong, an infectious disease previously unseen in human history. If not treated quickly, the patient could die of respiratory or multiple organ failure.

On December 12, 2002, a patient with an unusual case of pneumonia entered the Guangzhou Institute of Respiratory Diseases where Zhong Nanshan worked. The patient's symptoms were different from those of typical pneumonia, showing a continuous high fever and dry cough. The lungs showed "white lungs" through an X-ray fluoroscopy. Various antibiotics were ineffective.

As the patient's lungs had been acutely injured and his life was in danger, Zhong Nanshan tried a high-dose corticosteroid treatment and the patient recovered.

On January 2, 2003, it was reported that eight people who had come into previous contact with the patient in Heyuan, Guangdong Province were all infected with pneumonia with the same symptoms.

Zhong Nanshan was astonished. Based on his years of medical experience, he knew that this was a special infectious disease that deserved attention. He immediately reported this to his superiors.

Similar cases subsequently appeared in Zhongshan, Guangdong Province. At this critical juncture, Zhong Nanshan decided to go to Zhongshan to treat the patients along with a number of experts.

On January 22, 2003, this team comprising Zhong Nanshan and other medical experts prepared a formal written report on the investigation entitled

"Investigation Report on Pneumonia of Unknown Cause in Zhongshan", and they officially named the strange disease as Severe Acute Respiratory Syndrome (SARS). The report spelled out the clinical symptoms, treatment principles and preventive measures of SARS, and became an important document for guiding its diagnosis and treatment.

On February 18, 2003, Zhong Nanshan fell ill. He had been working straight for 38 hours, participating in continuous consultations, lectures, and various guidance activities. He had a high fever, cough and pneumonia. He had to stop working and receive medical treatment.

To avoid upsetting morale, he chose to go home to self-isolate for medical treatment instead of going to the Guangzhou Institute of Respiratory Diseases. There was no place to hang an infusion bottle at home, so he hammered a big nail into the door frame, which is still there today. While getting the home infusion, he studied medical records.

He said afterwards, "At that time, I wasn't sure if I'd survive. The left side of my chest was painful, and I was so weak that I was not able to carry a bowl. But I felt I couldn't give up. I had to live."

While he was ill, his wife Li Shaofen stayed by his side and took care of him. She later recalled, "He often didn't want to eat, and lost a lot of weight. I was very worried. In the past, I'd been an athlete and deputy captain of the basketball team. He helped me a lot. Now, my only priority is to help him."

Fortunately, Zhong Nanshan did not contract SARS, but rather a common pneumonia. An X-ray five days later showed that the shadow on his lungs had disappeared. As soon as his condition improved, he returned to the Guangzhou Institute of Respiratory Diseases to try to save the infected patients although he was weak.

Zhong Nanshan and his research team worked day and night, tackling key medical problems, and finally worked out a set of effective therapies, namely "three early and three reasonable measures" (early diagnosis, early isolation, and early treatment; reasonable use of corticosteroids, reasonable use of ventilators, and reasonable treatment of complications). They formulated a treatment plan with obvious curative effects.

The plan saved many critically ill patients and reduced the mortality rate. It would become the basic guideline for China's SARS diagnosis and treatment in the days to come, and played a key role in keeping the SARS mortality rate of Guangdong Province at the lowest level in China (3.8 percent) and China's overall SARS mortality rate at the low level of 6.6 percent in the world.

As of March 2003, the cumulative number of SARS cases reported in Guangdong Province had exceeded 1,000. The epidemic had spread though Guangdong Province, the country and even the world. Taking into account the medical experience of the Guangzhou Institute of Respiratory Diseases and the serious infectiousness of critically ill patients, Zhong Nanshan told the Guangdong Provincial Department of Health to "send all critically ill patients to the institute."

It was a powerful statement, resonating still today. Although he was 67 years old at that time, in the face of the epidemic he was still like a fighter rising to a challenge.

Chapter Eleven

Daring to Give Honest and Accurate Medical Information

In the early stage of the SARS epidemic, experts from the Chinese Center for Disease Control and Prevention suggested that the pathogen was chlamydia, and recommended antibiotic treatment.

Chlamydia is a microorganism with characteristics between bacteria and viruses, and the treatment for a chlamydia infection is different from that of a viral infection. If the therapy is wrong, it is likely to aggravate the patient's condition and delay recovery.

Zhong Nanshan could not agree with that. He publicly opposed the claim that the pathogen was chlamydia, insisting that it could be a virus.

He said afterwards, "The scientific statement was based on truth and facts. When comparing a statement based on scientific study to that from an authority, of course I respect the science, not the authority.... This is not a general academic discussion, but a life-saving issue."

At first, there were not many reports about SARS cases. It was not until April 2003 more and more reports of SARS cases appeared in China's official media.

Due to the lack of information about the disease, rumors began to spread, such as "treating SARS with white vinegar", and also triggered a panic buying wave of white vinegar and other goods in Guangzhou, rumored to help recovery. The panic buying also spread to other parts of the country.

Zhong Nanshan was anxious. He knew that the epidemic was spreading rapidly across the country.

If correct information was not disclosed as soon as possible, people would not be able to take correct prevention measures, and the epidemic would only get worse and worse.

On April 10, a press conference was held in Beijing for officials of the World Health Organization and Chinese and foreign journalists, and Zhong Nanshan was asked to attend. On the first day, Zhong Nanshan tactfully explained the current epidemic. "As an expert in this field, I think this disease can be controlled as long as patients are effectively isolated."

On the second day, a journalist asked him, "In your opinion, has the epidemic been kept under control so far?" Zhong Nanshan finally could no longer hold back. He said, "No, not at all."

The entire venue was in an uproar. Zhong Nanshan went on to say, "At present, I cannot say that the epidemic is controlled, but I can only say that it is contained. The precondition for controlling it is to discover the pathogen of the disease and find the treatment therapy. At present, the pathogen of this disease has not yet been determined, so how can I say that the epidemic is under control?"

Reports on the epidemic soon drew the attention of the leader of the Party Central Committee and the General Secretary, who supported the "international coordination."

On April 16, the World Health Organization officially announced that the pathogen of SARS (Severe Acute Respiratory Syndrome) was a new type of coronavirus and named it "SARS Coronavirus," confirming Zhong Nanshan's long-held view.

On April 20, the Minister of Health and the Deputy Secretary of Beijing Municipal Party Committee were dismissed due to their inability to effectively manage the response to SARS epidemic. This day was called "a milestone in rewriting China's fight against SARS."

Zhong Nanshan's persistence caused a fundamental change in China's fight against SARS. On April 21, the Ministry of Health introduced a daily public report system. On April 23, the State Council established the SARS Prevention and Control Headquarters to lead and coordinate the national SARS prevention and control work. These measures directed the fight against SARS onto the right track.

On July 2, the last three SARS patients from the First Affiliated Hospital of Guangzhou Medical College were diagnosed as having a full recovery and were discharged. China succeeded in fighting SARS. Zhong Nanshan and his team had worked for 193 days and treated 302 SARS cases. Not only did they set a record for the longest working hours during the SARS period, but they also achieved a discharge rate of 93 percent.

From July 13, 2003, there have been no new or suspected SARS cases reported anywhere in the world. The epidemic had ended.

Zhong Nanshan had worked on the frontline and made important contributions to achieving the victory in the battle against the epidemic, which won the respect and admiration of the Chinese people. He won many awards, such as National Model Worker, National Outstanding Party Member, National Health System Advanced Individual in Fighting SARS, National Norman Bethune Medal, Guangdong Model Party Member, Guangdong Medical Ethics Model, Guangdong Province's special meritorious service in fighting SARS, Guangzhou Advanced Individual in Fighting SARS, and the Guangdong Province special award for science and technology. In the face of the flowers and honors showered upon him, Zhong Nanshan was always modest, saying many times, "Actually, I am just a doctor."

On February 20, 2004, CCTV announced their selection of "Figures Who Moved China in 2003." Zhong Nanshan was elected with a high number of votes. In presenting the award, the announcer read, "In the face of the sudden outbreak of SARS, he remained calm and fearless, saving lives with a doctor's hands and responding to the disaster with a scientist's scientific attitude of seeking the truth from facts. He has said, 'In my position, doing a good job of preventing and curing diseases is the greatest political mission.' This forceful statement shows his outlook on life and his professional ethics. He empowered people to triumph over the epidemic with his admirable academic courage, noble medical ethics and in-depth scientific explorations."

Chapter Twelve

Constantly Making Progress

After SARS, Zhong Nanshan continued to work on the frontline of clinical practice and busied himself with outpatient services, consultations, and ward rounds. He also did not slacken his efforts in medical research. He led over 10 major research projects such as the Global Initiative for Chronic Obstructive Lung Disease by WHO, and published more than 540 SCI papers in international authoritative academic journals and more than 400 papers in national journals sponsored by the Chinese Medical Association and other institutions. He also published more than 20 medical books and obtained nearly 60 patents, including over 30 for utility models.

He has said, "No matter how good things are, if they can't be widely used in society, the process of their innovation will not end." He believes that scientific research calls for meeting basic needs as well as the highest standards. In other words, scientists should not only keep up with international cutting-edge concepts and work on tackling national urgent projects, but they should also satisfy the basic public need of developing effective, safe, inexpensive and convenient medical equipment and medicines.

Zhong Nanshan led his team in establishing a system by which enterprises, universities and research institutes could cooperate and coordinate through the State Key Laboratory of Respiratory Diseases which was working to develop drugs suited to China's national conditions and was forming new strategies for early prevention and treatment. He and his team found that carbocisteine, a commonly used cheap domestic expectorant, could significantly reduce the acute bout of COPD by 24.5 percent, thereby reducing the cost of conventional treatment of COPD by 85 percent. This paper, entitled "The Effect of Carbocisteine on Acute Exacerbation of Chronic Obstructive Pulmonary Disease (PEACE Study): A Randomized Placebo-Controlled Study," was published in The Lancet, the world's top medical journal in June 2008. It was selected as the Paper of 2008 by *The Lancet*. This was the first time for Chinese scientific researchers to win the honor.

In June 2009, Influenza A broke out in the Pearl River Delta of Guangdong, and Influenza A patients appeared all over the country. In March 2013, a new type of avian influenza known as H7N9 was found in Shanghai and Anhui Province, and cases were reported across the country. Zhong Nanshan and his team played a vital role in tackling these two new sudden respiratory infections.

For many years, Zhong Nanshan worked on the frontline in fighting epidemics. He also led his team in exploring and establishing a prevention and control system for severe respiratory infectious diseases in line with China's national conditions, and formed an internationally advanced "prevention-treatment-control" medical cycle chain management system for new and idiopathic serious respiratory infectious diseases. This has played an important role in promoting the establishment of China's public health prevention and control system, improving the ability and efficiency of serious epidemic detection and monitoring, and training emergency response personnel.

On many occasions, he informed people about public health emergencies in a timely manner. He has published many popular science articles on respiratory diseases, and has called on the general public to pay great attention to respiratory health through countless live broadcasts, special columns and lectures, and has strived to help the general public better understand necessary medical knowledge.

On December 18, 2018, the CPC Central Committee and the State Council awarded Zhong Nanshan the title of "Reform Pioneer", and he was elected as the "Important Figure Promoting the Establishment of the Public Health Emergency Response System".

Chapter Thirteen

Fighting the COVID-19 Epidemic

In December 2019, some hospitals in Wuhan, Hubei Province reported cases of pneumonia of an unknown cause with a connection to a local market known as the South China Seafood Market. The patients' early symptoms were similar to those of the flu, namely hypodynamia and coughing.

On December 26, Zhang Jixian, a doctor from Hubei Provincial Hospital of Integrated Traditional Chinese and Western Medicine, found that fever was not a necessary manifestation of this new type of pneumonia. Some patients had no fever, but had a dry cough, and they also had pathologic changes in their lungs. She reported these cases to the hospital, which immediately submitted a report to Jianghan District Center for Disease Control and Prevention on December 27. On December 29, Hubei and Wuhan Health Commissions instructed relevant CDCs and hospitals to carry out epidemiological research.

As the number of cases in Wuhan increased, the epidemic began to capture the attention of the country. Professor Zhong Nanshan, at that time an 84-year-old man, was appointed the leader of a high-level expert team formed by the National Health Commission.

On January 8, 2020, the team initially confirmed that a new coronavirus was the pathogen of the epidemic.

On January 11, the Chinese Center for Disease Control and Prevention uploaded the entire genome sequence of the new coronavirus to its website to share data with the world and the WHO.

But still, there were many questions. Was the epidemic SARS? Where was the pathogen? Was there evidence of human-to-human transmission? People were eager to hear from a scientific authority on the subject. That person was Zhong Nanshan.

When a journalist interviewed him, he gave advice to the general public: "In my opinion, don't go to Wuhan without a special reason."

However, on the evening of January 18, Zhong Nanshan was rushing to the epidemic frontline in Wuhan. Because it was the Spring Festival travel season, plane tickets were sold out. He bought a seatless high-speed rail ticket, but eventually found a seat in the dining car.

When he arrived that night, he rushed to the Wuhan Municipal Health Commission to learn more about the situation and began working immediately.

On the morning of January 19, he attended the epidemic seminar to hear the Wuhan Center for Disease Control and Prevention and the Health Commission give their reports on the epidemic. He then quickly went to the Wuhan Jinyintan Hospital where patients were receiving medical treatment and the Wuhan Center for Disease Control and Prevention. He did not have time to rest, and met with the other experts until 5 pm. Afterwards, he boarded a flight to Beijing. After arriving in Beijing at 10 pm, he immediately went to the National Health Commission for a meeting. When he returned to the hotel after the meeting, it was 2 o'clock in the morning.

On January 20, he confirmed human-to-human transmission of the new coronavirus when answering a question by a journalist. He reminded people to be vigilant and not go to Wuhan without a special reason. He also told people to go to a clinic if they had cold-like symptoms. He said it was important to wear masks when going out, and common masks could be used to prevent the spread of droplets if no N95 masks could be found. He also advised against eating game food since the pathogen was currently unknown, and could be from wild animals such as bamboo rats or badgers. Now people realized the virus was serious. Provinces initiated first-level responses, and the battle against the COVID-19 epidemic in China began.

On January 21, the Ministry of Science and Technology organized the First Meeting of the Scientific Research Team for the Joint Prevention and Control Mechanism of the COVID-19 Epidemic. The meeting announced the establishment of a scientific research expert team for the joint prevention and control of the COVID-19 epidemic which comprised 14 experts, with academician Zhong Nanshan as the team leader. From that moment, Zhong Nanshan began leading his team with the focus on providing clinical treatment while conducting scientific research.

On February 13, Zhong Nanshan's team announced the isolation of the novel coronavirus from the stool samples of COVID-19 patients.

On February 14, under the guidance of Zhong Nanshan, a rapid test kit for the novel coronavirus IgM antibody was developed by the State Key Laboratory of Respiratory Diseases and the Guangzhou Institute of Biomedicine and Health of the Chinese Academy of Sciences.

On February 28, Zhong Nanshan and more than 30 authors from across the country completed the research on "Clinical Features of China's 2019 Novel Coronavirus Infection" and published an article in the New England Journal of Medicine, the international medical journal. The research collected clinical information from about 1,099 confirmed patients from 552 hospitals in China and proposed immediate, strict epidemiological measures to curb the rapid spread of the epidemic.

On several occasions, Zhong Nanshan used telemedicine platforms to join the consultation for critically sick patients in Hubei and other parts of the country to reassure local doctors and patients. When discussing the cases with doctors on the frontline, he emphasized that no matter how sick patients are, the doctors must do their best to treat them and never give up.

The COVID-19 epidemic has been effectively controlled in China, but it is still severe in other parts of the world. Zhong Nanshan has been continuously working on the frontline of international medical research and sharing China's experience in fighting the epidemic.

He has said, "Infectious diseases know no borders. So long as even one country is not active in the fight, the global COVID-19 epidemic will not disappear."

Zhong Nanshan has had video conferences with international medical experts and representatives of missions in China to share experience in quarantine measures, case data and therapies, which all contributes to the global response to the epidemic.

"Through communication, other countries can avoid wrong detours," Zhong Nanshan said. "Because we have taken a difficult road, we must all support each other."

Because of infected arrivals from abroad, China's domestic epidemic resurged at the end of 2020. On January 25, 2021, 85-year-old academician Zhong Nanshan posted a 25-second video on a WeChat public account. It was only a few words, but it was very touching. In the video, he said, "The Spring Festival is the most important for family reunions in the hearts of the Chinese people, but this year thousands of Chinese people are choosing to stay put. It is amazing to see people sacrifice family reunions for epidemic prevention. I'm Zhong Nanshan and I'm in Guangzhou. I would like to thank you for not going home during the Spring Festival."

出版策划：王君校　韩　晖
统筹协调：付　眉　韩　颖　彭　博
责任编辑：陆　瑜
英文编辑：卢　敏
插画绘制：胡美慧
封面设计：智玖拾（成都）文化传媒有限公司
印刷监制：汪　洋

图书在版编目（CIP）数据

钟南山：汉英对照 / 刘小琳编著；卢敏翻译 . 北京：华语教学出版社，2021.4
（中国时代先锋人物）
ISBN 978-7-5138-2099-8

Ⅰ．①钟… Ⅱ．①刘… ②卢… Ⅲ．①钟南山—生平事迹 Ⅳ．① D263

中国版本图书馆 CIP 数据核字（2021）第 051941 号

中国时代先锋人物：钟南山

刘小琳　编著

卢　敏　翻译

*

© 华语教学出版社有限责任公司
华语教学出版社有限责任公司出版
（中国北京百万庄大街 24 号　邮政编码 100037）
电话：(86)10-68320585, 68997826
传真：(86)10-68997826, 68326333
网址：www.sinolingua.com.cn
电子信箱：hyjx@sinolingua.com.cn
北京虎彩文化传播有限公司印刷
2021 年（32 开）第 1 版
2023 年第 1 版第 4 次印刷
ISBN 978-7-5138-2099-8
003990